Happy Father's Day!

Dada Bear

Bello Enzo Bear book series

To Angelo Luigi Rosa

For exclusive information email osanna@artpotentials.org Call 800-223-6184

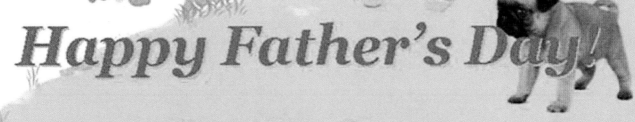

Happy Father's Day!

Dada Bear

Bello Enzo Bear book series

By Osanna M. Kazezian-Rosa
Photos and Illustrations by Osanna M. Kazezian-Rosa

Today is a happy day because it is Father's Day! Bello Enzo Bear is giving his Dada Bear a gift. A pug puppy!

Bello Enzo Bear likes to be outdoors, especially today! He is taking the new puppy for a walk!

Not too far from Bello Enzo Bear, are his sisters and Mama Bear.

Bella Bear and Emem Bear are gathering some flowers from the field along with Mama Bear!

Oh yes, Daisy their dog is tagging along too!

It is always fun for Bello Enzo Bear to roll down the green hills!

He is enjoying himself!

Watching the sheep graze!

I think the new puppy likes the frog!

Both Bello Enzo Bear and the puppy
are watching the frogs!

The puppy is feeling comfortable!

The puppy is having to pull his leg up to scratch.

"Oh puppy! You are scratching yourself!" said Bello Enzo Bear smiling.

Then, Bello Enzo Bear looked across the hill and saw his Dada Bear in the distance.

Dada Bear is walking towards Bello Enzo Bear.

With a big smile on his face, Bello Enzo Bear along with the pug puppy are looking towards Dada Bear.

He is waiving and shouting with joy!

"Dada! You have to come up here. See what I have for you!"

Dada Bear is surprised to see Bello Enzo Bear and the puppy. Dada Bear's favorite, a pug puppy!

Then Bello Enzo Bear said, "Dada this pug puppy is for you!"

"Oh! What a sweet puppy!" exclaimed Dada Bear, then he patted the puppy gently.

Dada Bear is patting the puppy!

"Bello Enzo Bear, thank you! You got me just what I always wanted to have when I was a young cub just like you, a pug puppy!" said Dada Bear smiling.

"Dada Bear what would you like to name your very own pug puppy?" asked Bello Enzo Bear.

"Bello Enzo Bear, I gather you are very fond of the new pug puppy!" commented Dada Bear smiling.

"Dada Bear smiling, responded and said, "Bello Enzo Bear please help me pick a name for the new puppy!"

Bello Enzo Bear smiled and said, "Ok, I will!"

Then, "Look Dada Bear, all the sheep are grazing now!" exclaimed Bello Enzo Bear.

"I enjoy watching the sheep eat their food. They are eating grass Dada Bear!" commented Bello Enzo Bear.

Dada Bear responded and said "Yes,
I see that Bello Enzo Bear. I guess it
is lunch time!"

Dada Bear continued and said, " How about we all go and have our lunch too, what do you say Bello Enzo Bear?"

"Yes! I am getting hungry too Dada Bear!" said Bello Enzo Bear.

Then! "Dada look! Mama and my sisters are coming towards us!" exclaimed Bello Enzo Bear with joy.

Daisy joined Bello Enzo Bear, his Dada Bear and the new puppy.

Mama Bear and her girls are joining
Dada Bear and Bello Enzo Bear!

Bello Enzo Bear is happy to see
Mama Bear and his sisters!

Dada Bear joined his loving family and they are heading back home to enjoy a healthy lunch together!

"Happy Father's Day Dada Bear!"
shouted the happy bunch.

About the author: Osanna M. Kazezian-Rosa is the creator of the children's picture books series: Bella Bear, Emem Bear and Bello Enzo Bear books.

Osanna has worked with young children in different settings.

"Happy Father's Day Dada Bear!" is the author's eighteenth book and the first in Bello Enzo Bear children's picture book series.

Most recent published work of the author is "Bella Bear My Friend Sophie's Art". Other publications of the author are the Bella Bear picture book series and Emem Bear picture books.

Bella Bear series is the author's first children's picture book collection which includes: "Bella Bear, My Cousin Candy Bear", "Bella Bear, It is My birthday!", "Bella Bear, My Little Brother-Bello Enzo Bear", "Bella Bear Picking Berries", "Bella Bear; I am a Big Sister", "Bella Bear's Family Portrait", "Bella Bear's Balloon Ride", "Bella Bear's Spring Time Picnic" 1st volume , "Bella Bear It is Summer Time" 2nd volume, "Bella Bear, It is Autumn" 3rd volume , " Bella Bear It is Winter Time-Let us go Skiing!" 4th volume in the season's books and "Bella Bear Our Big Ship Ride!"

Emem Bear is the second series of picture books collection published by the author which includes: "My Cousin Tiger Bear Likes To Read", "Emem Bear Likes Bubble Bath!" and "Emem Bear, Is two Years Old!".

Osanna also authored and published an instructional base unit entitled "The Art of Hand-Built Pottery; One Child's Creativity".

Osanna has earned a BA in History and Minor in Philosophy from UCLA. And MA in Education/Curriculum Teaching & Learning from Sonoma State University.

Made in the USA
Columbia, SC
13 August 2022

65281577R00024